Original title:
In the Arms of Winter

Copyright © 2024 Creative Arts Management OÜ
All rights reserved.

Author: Eleanor Prescott
ISBN HARDBACK: 978-9916-94-574-2
ISBN PAPERBACK: 978-9916-94-575-9

## In the Quiet of the Frost

Snowflakes swirl like little dancers,
Chilling noses, giving laughter glances.
Hot cocoa spills, it's a winter fight,
With marshmallows flying, oh what a sight!

Squirrels in sweaters, a fashion faux pas,
Chasing their tails, oh, what a bizarre.
Snowmen frown when carrots go missing,
While kids nearby are giggling and kissing.

Frosty breath floats like tiny white clouds,
As parents shake their heads, feeling proud.
Why wear a hat when hair can look wild?
Winter's a playground for every child.

So let's bundle up for this snowy spree,
With boots on our feet, come dance with me.
Together we'll laugh till the day is done,
For fun in the cold is just too much fun!

## Shadows of the Withered Leaves

Squirrels dance with acorn hats,
While birds sneak snacks from winter's mats.
A leaf slips by, it makes a sound,
Like whispers lost in woodlands found.

Cold winds chuckle, tickling cheeks,
Snowmen gossip, sharing freaks.
With frozen branches, trees do sway,
A frosty ballet, come what may.

## Heartbeats Beneath the Ice

Puddles freeze, a slipping spree,
Oh watch your step! It's slippery!
Yet laughter echoes, fun's not gone,
As winter shows us how to fawn.

A snowflake lands on someone's nose,
As fluffy jackets hide our woes.
Chasing snowballs, quick as light,
Who knew cold could feel so bright?

## Starlit Breezes and Frosted Fields

Frosty breath like clouds we puff,
While pet dogs try to look all tough.
Their tails wag fast, the chase is on,
Paw prints trailing 'til they're gone.

Stars wink down from chilly skies,
As giggles float where silliness lies.
We trip on ice, yet wear a grin,
The joy of winter's playful spin.

## Winding Paths in Crystal Worlds

Boots pound down on crunchy snow,
While snowflakes dance, put on a show!
Around we twirl, in circles amiss,
A feature we call winter bliss.

Branches laden with sugar white,
Snowball fights bring endless delight.
We laugh so hard, our cheeks turn red,
Who knew chill could fill us with dread?

## **Shivering Under Starry Skies**

Beneath the stars, we freeze and squeal,
In coats so thick, we barely feel.
We dance around like awkward ducks,
And laugh at ice, oh what bad luck!

The snowflakes fall, a soft, white kiss,
We tumble down, we can't find bliss.
With every slip, we squeal in glee,
As frostbite bites, oh woe is me!

## A Frosty Embrace of Memories

Hot cocoa mugs in chilly hands,
We reminisce on silly plans.
With marshmallows stuck on our nose,
Our laughter rings as winter froze.

We build a fort of snow and cheer,
But then we find a snowball near.
With giggles loud, we run and duck,
Our fortress falls, it's just our luck!

## Fields of White Silence

In fields so deep, our footprints trace,
Like penguins lost, we waddle, face.
The snow so deep, it tugs our shoes,
Yet we still giggle at our blues.

With snowmen stacking up so high,
We tip them over, oh my, oh my!
With carrot noses flying around,
We burst with laughter, tumbling down!

## Touched by the Breath of Frost

The world, a blanket, crisp and bright,
We chase our breath in frosty light.
In mittens thick, we throw some snow,
Our fingers numb, we still won't go.

With each small flake that lands and twirls,
We madly swirl like little girls.
In winter's thrall, we find our way,
In giggles lost, we play all day!

## **Solstice Secrets Unraveled**

Snowflakes are falling, a dance in the air,
Squirrels are plotting, they think we don't care.
Hats on our heads, we look quite absurd,
Chasing our children, as snowballs are stirred.

Frosty the snowman has hatched out a scheme,
To steal all our carrots, it's more than a dream.
We laugh as we slip on the slick icy ground,
With giggles and snickers, our joy knows no bound.

## Beneath the Winter Moon

Beneath the bright glow of a silvery light,
The penguins are waddling, oh what a sight!
They slide and they trip, throwing snow in the air,
As hot cocoa brews in the chill of despair.

The moon's got a grin, it knows all our games,
While we sing off-key, it laughs at our names.
Ice skates are twirling, a ballet gone wrong,
We dance like the snowflakes, where do we belong?

## Hushed Echoes of Frost

The world is a wonder, a cold comedy,
With mittens mismatched, it's a sight to see.
The hot soup is steaming, but oh, what a splash!
We wear spicy mustaches made out of ash.

The chilly wind whispers, "You're all my friends",
As we toss snowballs that never quite ends.
Laughter erupts with each playful throw,
As we build the best snow-castles, we know.

## A Tapestry of Cold

Under the blanket of soft, glimmering frost,
We build a snow fort, but oh, what a cost!
Each puff of white fluff is a reason to grin,
As the dogs join the party, let the shenanigans begin!

Our noses are red, like Rudolph the dear,
The wintertime antics fill hearts with good cheer.
With cocoa in hand and snowflakes in hair,
We dance to the rhythm of winter's sweet air.

## Shadows of a Frosty Twilight

The snowflakes dance like tiny jesters,
Whirling round the frosty testers.
A snowman grins with a carrot nose,
Sipping cocoa as the cold wind blows.

Icicles hang like frozen swords,
While penguins play card games, not bored.
Yet here I am, bundled up tight,
Wishing for warmth, a sunny delight.

## The Embrace of a Frozen World

A penguin slipped on ice and fell,
Squeaking loudly, 'Oh, what the hell!'
Chasing snowflakes, the dogs will race,
Their fuzzy hats a silly embrace.

Frosty fingers on my nose,
I've lost my mittens, I suppose!
The snow is deep, my boots are hide,
Why do I venture out? I can't abide!

## Snowflakes in a Quiet Convo

Two snowflakes chat as they take a plunge,
Swapping tales of winter's grunge.
One says, 'I'm tired of all this white!',
The other snickers, 'At least we're light!'

We giggle at the shivers we share,
While icicles dangle, with frosty flair.
A squirrel in a scarf tries to make a call,
"Hey, winter buddy, mind if I stall?"

## Embracing the Bitter Breeze

The wind whispers jokes that freeze with glee,
Telling tales of the brave and silly tree.
Snowflakes slide down without a care,
Wishing they could find a warm pair!

My nose is red, like a cherry bright,
As snowmen hold hands in a chilly fight.
I wonder if they'll ever get warm,
Or just stay cold and cause a storm!

## **Frosted Leaves**

Leaves are dressed in icy coats,
They slip and slide like clumsy goats.
Squirrels in hats, they laugh aloud,
As winter wraps the trees in clouds.

Snowmen grinning with carrot noses,
Waving at the children in frozen poses.
Hot cocoa spills as children race,
To catch the snowflakes, a chilly chase.

## **Silent Stories**

Snowflakes whisper on the ground,
As snowball fights make leaps and bounds.
The cat in boots, prancing around,
Chasing shadows with no sound.

The dog flips over, stuck like glue,
Wondering what to do or chew.
Lost mittens tell tales of glee,
As winter spins its frosty spree.

## **In the Blanket of Winter**

Blankets piled, a cozy mound,
Under layers, laughter's found.
Hot pies warm the frosty air,
As giggles dance without a care.

Gnarled trees wear fluffy socks,
Dodging snowballs, forgetting clocks.
If penguins could play cards, you'd see,
A festive game with no referee!

## Singing to the Snowflakes

Belles of winter, they float and twirl,
Children shout as the snowflakes swirl.
A snowman sings with frosty cheer,
While birds in hats have no fear.

Guitar strings made of icicles,
Strumming tunes beneath the swirls.
Snowballs launched, a musical fight,
As snowmen dance into the night.

## Embracing the Frosted Solstice

A party planned with frosty bliss,
But someone slipped and fell with a hiss.
Laughter fills the air like spice,
As we toast to winter, oh so nice!

With every snowflake, a joke unfolds,
Tales of warmth in the winter cold.
Fingers numb but hearts alight,
Dancing on frost, what a sight!

## The Silence of Falling Snow

Snowflakes dance like awkward sprites,
Hiding from the sun's bright bites.
They tumble down with giggles light,
Creating chaos in soft white sights.

Snowmen plotting in the night,
Arms of twig, they start to fight.
With carrots as their clever eyes,
They scheme beneath the cloudy skies.

Icicles hanging, jagged tales,
Catch the laughter on winter gales.
With every chill, the joy unveils,
Frosty whispers where fun prevails.

So let us laugh, for time will show,
That winter's charm is much like snow.
A blanket silly, soft, and bright,
Brings giggles forth in pure delight.

## Ghosts of Warmth Past

Remember when the sun was bold?
And every ice cream cone was gold?
Now we sip on soups so hot,
While dreaming of the warmth we've not.

Sweaters stuffed with memories bright,
Pantless days lost to the night.
Now we clutch our tea with glee,
Shivering, but don't let it be.

Look, a mug, a cozy friend,
With marshmallows we pretend.
Each fluffy ghost, a summer whim,
Yet here we sit, our light growing dim.

Winter's whims may cause some fright,
But joy's the heart, wrapped warm and tight.
With ghosts of sun and laughter past,
We toast to memories that hold steadfast.

## Enchanted by the Chill

The biting air gives quite a thrill,
As snowflakes whirl in topsy swill.
Each gust of wind a jolly tease,
That tickles noses, brings us to knees.

Squirrels in hats, what a sight!
Chasing each other in pure delight.
The trees are dressed in coats of white,
Whispering secrets in frosty light.

Hot chocolate on a snowy day,
With whipped cream clouds leading the way.
We laugh and slip, oh what a show,
As winter's charm makes giggles grow.

Embrace the cold with silly cheer,
For frosty nights are drawing near.
So dance around, let spirits spill,
We're all enchanted by this chill.

## Serenity Wrapped in White

Wrapped in blankets, snug and tight,
While outside, battles rage and fight.
Snowball wars in neighbors' backyards,
Where laughter echoes, no one's on guard.

The world transforms to winter's play,
With every flake that drifts away.
Who knew being cold could be so fun?
We count the snowflakes, one by one.

Yet inside cookies start to bake,
With every munch, we giggle and quake.
The aroma floats, it hugs like a wink,
While outside, hot cocoa makes us think.

So here we sit, and giggles swell,
In this fluffy white, oh can't you tell?
Serenity reigns, though weird and tight,
Wrapped in wonder, snugged up right.

## The Chill of Silence

The snowflakes dance with glee,
As I slip on my slippery spree.
Snowmen wobble, hats askew,
I swear they're laughing, too.

The air is cold, my breath is puffs,
Hot cocoa's gone, oh, that's tough!
My nose turns red, like Rudolph's side,
At least my sweater is winter-tied.

The dog leaps high, with joy he bounds,
But lands in snow; there's no more ground.
I chuckle loud, a frosty cheer,
Who knew winter brought such fear?

With teeth that chatter, I brace the chill,
Yet every moment brings a thrill.
Embrace the frost, let laughter flow,
Winter's a joke, that tickles the toe!

# Beneath a Blanket of White

A blanket draped on slumbering streets,
Where snowmen wear their carrot treats.
Kids slide down hills, squeals and yells,
While snowballs launch like tiny spells.

My hat is lost to the icy breeze,
Mittens vanish, where's the peace?
I trudge along, a snow-clad mess,
Looking like an unkempt dress.

Hot cocoa spills; oh, what a fate!
Marshmallows floating, on my plate.
I sip, then smile, with goo on my chin,
Winter's charm, like a playful grin.

The sun peeks through, a cheeky beam,
Melting snow, it's a wacky dream.
Let's build a fort and have a fight,
Beneath this blanket, all feels right!

## Surrender to the Snowfall

As snowflakes tease, I lose my grace,
I sweep and slip in this frozen place.
With every step, I wobbly hop,
Might as well aim for a tumble flop.

Frosty air, with laughter loud,
A snow angel forms beneath the cloud.
I thrash about, the white stuff gleams,
Am I an angel? I have my dreams.

A snowball flies, my aim is poor,
It hits the mailbox, shuts the door.
The dog just barks in sheer delight,
As I construct my next snowfight.

In cozy clothes, we gather 'round,
With chattering teeth, a merry sound.
Embrace the chilly, glitchy ball,
What fun it is to surrender, after all!

## Solstice Serenade

The light is dim, the nights are long,
I belt out notes in a winter song.
The cats all stare, they think I'm mad,
But I'm just jiving, isn't it rad?

With scarves so bright, I strut and sway,
Like a penguin on parade today.
My neighbors peek from curtain seams,
Are they impressed, or lost in dreams?

The snowman's grin is quite absurd,
Did he just wink? That's so unheard!
I break into dance, twirl and spin,
In this snowy stage, I'll always win.

Through frosty nights beneath moon's glow,
I'll dance and sing, let laughter flow.
So raise your glass, give winter cheer,
Our funny times bring warmth so near!

## **Reveries in the Glittering Cold**

Snowflakes dance like silly clowns,
Throwing sparkles all around.
My nose is red, my cheeks like plums,
As frostbite hits, I mumble 'bums!'

Hot cocoa spills, a chocolate dream,
Marshmallows float, a sugary beam.
But wait, what's that? A rogue snowball!
I duck and dodge—oh, winter's call!

Boots that squeak, like rubber ducks,
I wobble, tumble, oh, what luck!
Snowman grins with a carrot nose,
He looks like he needs a stylish pose!

So here's to frosty, whimsical cheer,
With snaps and crackles, winter's here!
We'll giggle 'til the sun breaks through,
And find more fun than we ever knew!

## Frosted Whispers of the Night

The moon is snickering, shining bright,
As icy gales take off in flight.
Penguins slide in comical haste,
While snowmen stare, with frosty taste.

Twirling with glee on frozen ground,
Frolicsome fun is always found.
Snowflakes tumble like furry cats,
Avoiding hats and squeaky mats.

A snowball fight goes wildly wrong,
With laughter echoing, oh so strong.
I trip and fall in a frosty heap,
While winter giggles, not a peep.

So, grab your sled, let's make a scene,
We'll race the winds, so crisp and keen.
And when the chill begins to bite,
We'll laugh and play till morning light!

## Embrace of the Snowfall

A snowy blanket, fluff and white,
Cats are plotting stealthy flight.
While I chase after a runaway glove,
Silly adventures, oh, how we shove!

Frosty noses, hot breath like steam,
Winter's antics—oh, what a dream!
Snowflakes tickle like tiny feet,
As we dance in a frosty beat.

Sleds zoom by, laughter fills the air,
Cocoa in hand, without a care.
But who threw that? Was it you, my friend?
A fluffy showdown that has no end!

So let's embrace this frosty spree,
Chasing the whims of wintery glee.
With cheeks aglow and spirits high,
We'll conquer cold, you and I!

## A Chilling Serenity

Bundled up like a marshmallow treat,
I trudge through snow with clumsy feet.
Ice cubes jingle in my coat,
While penguins cheer, 'Don't let us gloat!'

The squirrels play leapfrog in the snow,
While I fumble, feeling quite slow.
Snowflakes whisper little jokes,
As I dodge them like playful folks.

With cocoa fish and cookie bears,
We've brewed up some wintery flares.
Felons of frost, we won't complain,
Just sprinkle joy, like snowy rain.

A winter's whimsy, full of delight,
With giggles echoing through the night.
So here we'll bask in frosty fun,
Until the dawn—our laughter won!

## The Softness of Frozen Nights

Snowflakes dance like tiny clowns,
Covering rooftops, hiding frowns.
There's laughter in the chilly air,
As mittens vanish without a care.

Hot cocoa spills from mugs in haste,
Sipping it down with a frosty taste.
We're wrapped like burritos, snug and tight,
In cozy sweaters, oh what a sight!

Icicles dangle, sharp and bright,
Pretending they're swords in a winter fight.
But during the snowball skirmish we see,
The real champion is the hot soup, whee!

So bring on the snow, let it gleam,
We'll build our castles, let's all daydream.
With giggles aplenty and warmth all 'round,
In this frozen kingdom, joy is found.

## Chilled Moments of Reflection

A penguin waddles on the ice,
He slips and tumbles, oh how nice!
The snowman grins with a carrot nose,
While frozen fingers compose some prose.

Winter's chill brings thoughts so loud,
Who knew a scarf could feel so proud?
With each breath, a puff of mist,
I think of all the cookies missed!

We walk like robots, stiff yet spry,
While trees wear coats that make them shy.
And as we slip on roads of glass,
The laughter grows, time seems to pass.

With every laugh, the cold's undone,
For in this freeze, we still have fun.
So let us dance 'neath the twinkling stars,
In the quiet, we'll banish the winter scars.

**Frost's Tender Touch**

The frost arrived like an artist's brush,
Painting the world in a frosty hush.
Stretched out beds with blankets nice,
Dreaming of summer, oh isn't that spice?

Sleds zoom by, squeals fill the air,
While laughter bursts like a snowflake flare.
No sense in slipping, just let it go,
Then right back up for another snow show!

Snow angels spread their chilly wings,
As if they've come to see what joy brings.
And cocoa spills, but what the hay,
That only means it's time for play!

From icicle castles to chilly swings,
This icy season has the cutest things.
So come join the fun, let's build our glee,
With snowball fights, oh, wild and free!

## Seasons of Icicles and Dreams

Icicles hang like glassy teeth,
Daring snowflakes to dance beneath.
We hide from wind, we shiver and sway,
Yet with each moment, we find our way.

Hot chocolate laughter fills the room,
As winter's breath begins to bloom.
Pinecone soldiers in a crafty queue,
Who told a pine tree to wear a shoe?

The days are short, yet our spirits rise,
As we cradle the warmth despite the skies.
Frosty landscapes turn bright and bold,
With stories of joy and winter told.

So let the chill tickle our cheeks,
With every snowfall, the fun peaks.
In this frosty realm, we'll leap and glide,
For winter's laughter is our guide!

## **The Heart of a Frostbitten World**

Frosty breath in the air, so crisp,
Snowflakes dance like they're on a trip.
Socks on hands, just call it style,
Waddling outside, it's all worth the while.

Chill nips at noses, cheeks turning red,
Sleds soar high, that's the fun we've bred.
Hot cocoa spills on a frigid floor,
Laughter echoes, we can't take it anymore.

Icicles dangle, ready to fall,
Laughter bubbles, we thrill and we sprawl.
Each winter game, a slip or a fall,
In the frosty grip, we're having a ball.

Bundled tight in layers, looking like peas,
Falling down softly, we're tickled by these.
The joy of the season is perfectly clear,
In our silly antics, we've nothing to fear.

## **Winter's Velvet Touch**

Snowball fights bring out our giggles,
With icy hands, we conjure our wiggles.
Slipping on ice, what a graceful show,
Humor shines bright in the moon's frosty glow.

Sipping soup feels like a warm embrace,
Chasing squirrels quickens up the pace.
Mittens lost in the deepest of drifts,
Where's the match? It gives us all great lifts.

Snowmen with noses of the carrot kind,
Snowflakes whisper secrets we can't find.
With every tumble, we enter a trance,
Dancing with snowflakes, all in good chance.

In the frosty air, our laughter ignites,
Winter's gentle touch, pure delight in sights.
Sharing the silliness, we all agree,
This chilly spectacle's the best, with glee.

## A Symphony of Hushed Snowfall

Whispers of flakes fall soft and slow,
Covering the world like a fluffy pillow.
Tripping over boots, who needs to run fast?
As we roll in the snow, we're having a blast.

Silent streets, but laughter rings clear,
Falling into snowbanks, no need for fear.
Mittens mismatched, we embrace the fun,
Creating our magic under winter's sun.

Making snow angels, wings far and wide,
Chasing around with joy as our guide.
Frosty eyebrows like a frozen art piece,
In a chilly world, we find our release.

Every snowflake's a joke that's unsaid,
Creating memories in our frosty bed.
The beauty around is sleek and surreal,
In the hush of the season, we laugh and we squeal.

## Emotions Enfolded in Ice

Clambering outside with a colorful coat,
Puffed up like marshmallows, we float.
Snowmen are wobbly, but proud as can be,
With eyes made of buttons, do they see me?

Winter snickered as we pulled out our sleds,
Diving down hills, laughing till we're red.
The cold may bite, but our hearts feel warm,
In this snowy madness, it's quite the charm.

Hot tea's steaming, we gather around,
With tales of the frosty, dear winter ground.
Accidental falls become legends we share,
For each tumble taken, there's joy in the air.

Wrapped in our layers, we shuffle and slip,
Each frosty moment, we joyfully grip.
With smiles and giggles, let future ones write,
In a world wrapped in ice, we twinkle so bright.

## **Where Quietness Meets the Chill**

Snowflakes dance like little clowns,
Wearing all their fluffy gowns.
A snowman with a carrot nose,
Singing loudly, nobody knows!

Icicles hang like teeth in a grin,
Waiting for a brave bird to begin.
Hot cocoa spills, laughter so sweet,
In this frosty land, it's a treat!

Snowball fights and slippery floors,
Rolling down hills, we yell for more!
Unruly trousers, frozen feet,
We chuckle at this chilly feat!

By the fire, tales are spun,
Of frosty giants who just want fun.
With each chilly breath, we exclaim,
Winter's antics, a joyful game!

## A Canvas of Winter's Embrace

The world is painted white and bright,
Where snowflakes giggle in pure delight.
Trees wear coats of snowy fluff,
While raccoons in hats say, 'That's enough!'

Snowmen chatter, their smiles wide,
Trying to give each other a ride.
Penguins waddle with swagger and flair,
Making snow angels without a care!

Each gust of wind brings frosty cheer,
As winter squirrels hide their loot near.
A blizzard's whisper, a joke on us,
Yet we laugh at winter's fuss!

In cozy blankets, we watch the show,
As the snowflakes dance to and fro.
In every flake, a grin might hide,
Laughter and winter, side by side!

## Cradled in White Silence

Under soft blankets of white froth,
A snowflake breaks out, says, 'Oh, bother!'
With winter's breath, so crisp and bold,
A sock slips off; my toes feel cold!

Kids with bright boots dash and play,
Chasing snowballs all through the day.
'Catch me if you can!' they scream with glee,
While the dog pulls me, oh, what a spree!

Laughter echoes in a frozen glee,
As snow drifts pile up like a spree.
Hot chocolate spills; oh, what a mess!
In winter's grip, we feel so blessed!

Stillness brushes the world with care,
As we giggle at snowflakes in the air.
Frosty whispers, a sweet embrace,
Winter's magic, a funny face!

## When Earth Holds its Breath

With the hush of snow, the world is still,
But hilarity hides behind the chill.
A family of deer, just peeking through,
Wearing tiny scarves, do they think it's new?

The air is crisp and crispier too,
As I slip and slide, who knew?
Snow pants crinkle, a curious noise,
While I dodge the snowballs thrown by boys!

Every flake seems to giggle and tease,
As chilly breezes tickle the trees.
The snowflakes swirl in a merry dance,
Inviting us all to join the chance!

By evening glow, we'll recount the day,
With laughter and warmth in a cuddly way.
Through snowball fights and drifts that rise,
Winter wraps us in funny surprise!

## Embraced by the Arctic Breath

Frosty toes and icy noses,
Chasing snowflakes, in warm poses.
Woolly hats with ears so grand,
Falling down, we make a stand.

Sledding down the hill with speed,
But landing face-first, oh dear me!
Snowman smiles, they wave hello,
Sometimes they melt, but that's the show.

## Serenity of the Snowy Dawn

Morning light in snowy robes,
Sipping cocoa, twirling probes.
Squirrels dance in fluffy gear,
While I trip over my own rear.

A snowball fight, oops, a miss!
"Hacked a Yeti!" that's my bliss.
Chortles echo throughout the park,
Frostbitten laughs, warm hugs embark.

## The Stillness of Fallen Flakes

Whispers soft as snowflakes paste,
 Laughter hiding, what a waste!
 Kick the snow, let chaos reign,
You'll find no reason for this pain.

A cat in a knitted hat, so sly,
 Prowling in snowdrifts, oh my!
Frosty paws, they prance, beware!
While we watch, we stop and stare.

## An Elegy for the Cold Moon

Frosted glass and chilly snacks,
How many layers 'til I crack?
Moonlit strolls that make me freeze,
Counting layers, with a sneeze!

Icicles hanging, look so cool,
And yet I shiver like a fool.
But laughter warms the frozen night,
If I trip again, it'll be all right.

## **Veil of the Silent Storm**

The snowflakes dance with pretty flair,
As squirrels slip in their fluffy hair.
A snowman grins with a carrot nose,
While kids build forts in their winter clothes.

Hot cocoa spills while laughter rings,
The dog dashes out, oh the chaos brings!
Chasing his tail, he slips and falls,
Snowballs flying from five-year-olds' squalls.

On the rooftops, icicles gleam,
As folks play chess, but it's a frozen scheme.
"Checkmate!" they cry, as pieces slide,
The king takes a tumble, with icy pride.

With each frosty breath, they puff and play,
Creating new games in the soft white display.
In this chilly realm, where giggles collide,
Joy runs rampant, oh what a ride!

# Beneath the Silvery Veil

Under a blanket of soft, white cheer,
Snowmen dance and drink some beer.
The cat leaps, but lands in a flop,
While birds gossip from the treetops atop.

A snowball fight turns into a snow-splash,
With mittens flying, it's a wild clash.
"Hey, that's unfair!" one child will say,
As laughter echoes, drifting away.

The ice on the pond, a slippery trap,
Skaters zig-zag with a comic flap.
"Look at me glide!" one skater yells,
Then down they go, tangled like bells.

Yet through the blizzard, a warmth we find,
In goofy giggles, and hearts entwined.
So bring on the snow, and all that it brings,
With funny tales and the joy winter sings!

## A Whisper of Winter's Touch

The trees wear coats of icy lace,
While rabbits hop in a hilarious chase.
A crow lands heavy on a slim branch,
And the whole thing shakes; what a quirky chance!

Children twirl in their knitted gear,
Slipping and sliding, they'll grab a beer.
Snowflakes fall like feathers from birds,
As doggies jump and pounce like nerds.

Hot soup simmers, but spills on the floor,
While dad cries, "Where's the ladle, oh more!"
Mom laughs as the puppies make mess,
Winter can't stop this charming excess!

Through frostbitten cheeks and red noses bright,
Laughter and warmth glow in the night.
So let winter sprinkle its goofy delight,
For joy's the real magic that keeps us upright!

## Footprints in the Snow's Soft Blanket

Footprints trail like a wobbly dance,
As penguins march, giving snow a chance.
The dog takes off like a furry brick,
While kids yell, "Wait, we haven't picked!"

Snowballs whiz with shrieks of glee,
One hits dad, and oh, what a spree!
"You've declared war!" he dramatically cries,
But all he can do is join in the pies.

A snow globe shakes under children's hands,
With each little twist, a blizzard expands.
The cat, confused, gives a curious meow,
As kids stack snow like a towering cow.

When morning breaks with a soft, warm glow,
They recount their folly from last night's show.
In this wintry wonder, let laughter reign,
For smiles and snowflakes are never in vain!

## **A Dance of Ice and Breath**

Snowflakes swirl, a flurry of glee,
Chasing my dog, who's chasing me!
A slip, a slide, a giggling fall,
Oh winter's mischief, it beckons us all.

Hot cocoa spills, marshmallows fly,
Chasing each other, we leap and sigh.
With hats askew and scarves askance,
We tumble together, in snow we prance.

Icicles dangling, sharp as can be,
Daring the kids to climb up a tree.
But one slip later, what's that we hear?
A thump from the snow, and a raucous cheer!

So let's all twirl, let's all embrace,
This chilly season, with a smiling face.
Because laughter echoes in frosty air,
Winter's whimsy, a play we all share.

## The Quiet Majesty of Cold

Frost bites noses, with icy flair,
While penguins huddle for warmth to share.
Woolly hats like boulders on heads,
Taking snow selfies, while sipping on spreads.

Snowmaps written with footprints galore,
Oh look, there's a snowman - wait, is that a door?
Kids in the yard, the base our delight,
Declare it a castle, then reign with might!

Sleds in a lineup, like cars on a street,
One brave kid bold, says, "Let's take the seat!"
Downhill they roll, with laughter and scream,
The majesty of cold, more fun than a dream!

So let's bundle up, let's hit the ground,
In this wintry kingdom, laughter is found.
With snowflakes falling like confetti from skies,
We'll toast to the cold, with bright, joyful cries!

**Wrapped in Crystal Dreams**

Twinkling lights dance upon the snow,
As frostbite ninjas put on a show.
Snowballs exchanged, more hits than misses,
And laughter erupts, igniting warm kisses.

Building a fortress with icy bricks,
Watch out! Here comes a flying mix!
A surprise attack; oh what fun it seems,
As we tumble together, lost in our dreams.

Giant snowflakes whisper, "Come out and play,"
Searching for adventures, we make our way.
In this winter magic, we frolic and scheme,
Wrapped in fun, like the best of dreams!

So let's cherish the chill, embrace the freeze,
With hot chocolate smiles and snow-kissed trees.
For in these cold days, we warmth will glean,
In laughter and joy, wrapped in crystal sheen.

# The Lullaby of a Winter Night

As stars twinkle in the chilly sky,
We whisper tales, and the puppies sigh.
A blanket of snow, soft as a dream,
Where laughter and joy make the dark glimmer and beam.

Frosty windows create secret scenes,
Of snowmen dancing in jeans and greens.
Hot cider in hand, we toast to the night,
In winter's embrace, everything feels right.

Dreams of sugarplums – well, that's what they say,
But really it's snowballs that lead us astray.
With giggles and tucks, the night wears a crown,
We drift off to sleep, no need for a frown.

So let's close our eyes, snug under the cover,
This winter's lullaby warms hearts like a lover.
For in this chill, we find heartwarming light,
With dreams full of laughter in the quiet of night.

## As Frost Claims the Earth

The ground wears a blanket of white,
Squirrels in jackets, what a sight!
They dance and leap, a comical show,
While frozen grass makes them go slow.

Chill nips at noses, cheeks so red,
Penguin waddles to bed, well-fed.
Snowmen stand tall with goofiest grins,
Arms made of twigs, and buttons for chins.

Hot cocoa spills, marshmallows fly,
Cupboard raiders make a sweet pie.
A snowball fight erupts with glee,
Laughing, falling, like leaves from a tree.

Winter's a prankster, can't you see?
It tosses us snowballs with great glee.
But we embrace this frosty cheer,
And toast to the laughter we hold dear.

## Slumbering Trees in Purity

The trees wear crowns of frosty lace,
But squirrels think it's a perfect place.
They burrow in deep, a cozy retreat,
Dressed up in winter, isn't that neat?

Branches creak softly, a funny sound,
As twigs play music upon the ground.
Each snowy whisper tells a tale,
Of trees in pajamas, who can't set sail.

Birds wear coats of fluffy delight,
And snuggle up tight to avoid frostbite.
They chirp silly tunes, a winter's song,
While the whole frozen world hums along.

Under this quilt, dreams quietly sway,
In slumber they chuckle, come what may.
Nature's a comedian, dressed in white,
With giggles echoing through the night.

## The Whispering Winds of December

The wind sweeps in with a sneaky huff,
Whirling and twirling, oh so puffed up.
It breathes in giggles, whispers of fun,
Playing tag with the snow, just begun.

It tickles your nose, plays with your hair,
Turns your scarf into quite the dare.
With a whoosh and a woosh, it pulls on your coat,
Laughing aloud as you nearly float!

It gathers up leaves, and chases them round,
A cheeky little sprite, full of sound.
Whispers of winter escape in the breeze,
As giggles and chuckles dance with the trees.

So here we stand, in its playful wake,
Embracing the madness that winds can make.
December's laugh is clear as a bell,
A mischievous echo we know all too well.

## Glistening Memories of the Past

Snowflakes fall like popcorn from air,
Remembering days without a care.
With each gentle flake, we recall,
The sledding adventures, a glorious brawl.

Hot soup spills over from the big pot,
As laughter erupts, using all that we've got.
Grandma's old tales, so funny to hear,
Of snowball fights that still bring cheer.

With mittens mismatched and noses aglow,
The joy in our hearts begins to flow.
Memories shimmer like ice on the lake,
Wrap them in smiles, for goodness' sake!

So let's build a fort, have a snowball spree,
Capture the moments, let winter run free.
As we reminisce, let laughter be vast,
In this frosty season, hold tight to the past.

**Frost-Kissed Embrace**

Beneath a blanket, soft and white,
My cat stole my spot, oh what a plight!
He purrs with glee, all warm and round,
While I sit here, lost and confound.

The snowflakes tumble, they dance and swirl,
I venture out for a spin and twirl.
But socks are slippery, oh what a scene!
I end up face-first in snowy cuisine!

My nose is bright red, like a cherry, oh dear,
I laugh at my folly while friends disappear.
Snowball fights start, but I just duck,
Who knew winter could feel like such luck?

With cheeks all aglow and laughter so loud,
We chase each other, lost in the crowd.
Through frosty chaos, we find our way,
In this frozen wonderland, we just want to stay.

## Whispers of the Snowbound Heart

The wind whispers secrets, oh what a tease,
It tickles my ear and gives me a freeze.
I strive for romance in this chilly affair,
But my date slipped on ice, flew up in the air!

Fluffy snowmen line the neighborhood street,
With cartwheel hats and tiny cold feet.
They smile at me with a carrot grin,
As I sip hot cocoa, my new favorite sin.

Snowflakes are kisses, that float from the sky,
But when they land, they want to say bye!
They melt too quickly, what a cruel game,
Why can't they stay and remember my name?

Still, laughter erupts in the frosty expanse,
We twirl through the season, let's give it a chance.
With mittens all wet and cheeks all aglow,
We embrace the winter, let the good times flow!

## **Frosted Dreams and Cinder Skies**

Dreams of snowmen start to unfold,
As visions of frozen noses grow bold.
But as I build up, they fall with a thud,
My masterpiece melts into a puddle of crud!

Each winter morning is a race against time,
Get dressed for the cold? Oh, what a climb!
With layers galore and my boots on the wrong,
It's a comedy sketch; I cannot stay strong!

The cocoa I sip is a bit too hot,
While marshmallows dance like they're giving it a shot.
A sprightly snowball finds my favorite hat,
Who knew winter was such a silly spat?

Sledding downhill, it's a glorious ride,
But losing control? I'm off to the side!
With laughter echoing across the wide plains,
In these frosted dreams, pure joy reigns.

## **Where Icicles Weep**

Icicles hang like teeth from the eaves,
As I step outside, my breath it deceives.
I laugh at the chill, the brisk winter air,
But why does it feel like I'm almost bare?

With boots that squeak and a coat too big,
I trip over snowdrifts, that sneaky old fig.
A dance with the ice turns into a slide,
Who knew the ground could be such a ride?

My nose turns a shade of a bright rosy hue,
As I build a snow fort with rambunctious crew.
But snowballs are flung, and surprise starts to soar,
No one expects a full-on winter war!

Gloves soaked through, we laugh till we ache,
I need a warm hug, or maybe some cake.
In the chill of the moment, we find all the fun,
Where laughter erupts, and friendship's begun.

## Beneath the Veil of Ice

The snowman grins, his eyes are coal,
He seems to swallow winter's role.
Yet when the sun begins to shine,
He melts away like some fine wine.

His carrot nose starts to droop low,
"Not ready!" he screams, "Don't let me go!"
But with a laugh, the children shout,
"Next year, pal, we'll build you stout!"

The icicles hang like frozen spears,
Glistening sharp, they spark some fears.
Yet kids throw snowballs, they don't care,
And slide down hills without a care.

The winter cats in coats of cream,
Snuggle up and plot their dream.
To catch that pesky mouse or two,
But all they catch is frost and dew.

## **The Stillness After the Storm**

After the blizzard, silence reigns,
All is fluffy, soft like chains.
The world is wrapped, a giant cake,
We venture out, unsure, awake.

Kids in boots make monster tracks,
While adults clear the snow which stacks.
Yet once it settles, all is fun,
Until they slip, and down they run!

Sleds zoom past like planes on flight,
While dogs chase after, all delight.
Yet owners scream, "Not in my yard!"
While pups dig in, both brave and hard.

Laughter echoes through the streets,
Each slip and fall, a thousand feats.
The world transformed, it shines anew,
Even if a few pants got a view!

## Crystals of Solitude

The frosty window paints a scene,
With crystal patterns, soft and keen.
Inside we sip hot cocoa bliss,
While outside, squirrels hold a miss.

The trees wear coats of brilliant white,
As snowflakes dance, pure and light.
Yet one wrong step, a slip, a fall,
And suddenly you're part of it all!

With padded arms, we brave the chill,
Yet juggling snowballs is quite the thrill.
One aimed at you? You duck, you weave,
As laughter bursts, we all believe.

Through blizzards' gloom, we find our spark,
Creating joy despite the dark.
In solitude, we choose to play,
With snow and fun, we seize the day!

## **Winter's Soft Caress**

A snowflake whispers on my nose,
"I'm here to stay! Just thought you'd know!"
Yet as the sun begins to rise,
The warmth outside makes winter cry.

Fluffy mittens, mismatched too,
Fashion trends, oh yes, a few!
With scarves tangled, we chase our dreams,
While giggles echo through the beams.

The hot chocolate warms our hands,
While snowballs fly like small commands.
"Take that!" one shouts, "You can't escape!"
And waits for winter's next drape.

Though frost may bite and chill our toes,
The playful spirit simply grows.
With each soft touch of winter's play,
We laugh and dance the day away!

## Silent Breath of the Cold

Snowflakes dance like tiny sprites,
Chasing chickens, causing frights.
Icicles hang as sharp as knives,
Yet here we are, it's how we thrive.

Frosty air makes noses red,
While we cozy up in bed.
Hot cocoa spills on my warm lap,
I'm starting to feel like a winter sap.

Sledding down the hill we go,
But wait, I think I lost my toe!
With all the layers, I can't lift,
I might just be a walking gift.

As winter brings its chilly bite,
We laugh and play, it feels just right.
Through snowball fights and snowman feats,
Bundle up, and bring the treats!

## **Frost-kissed Dreams**

Pine trees wearing coats so grand,
Look like they're at a fancy stand.
Snowflakes whisper, 'Don't you dare!'
I bet they're plotting in the air.

A snowman smiles with a carrot nose,
But is it him or just his pose?
With every gust, he starts to sway,
I'm betting on him, what do you say?

Winter socks, oh how they creep,
Like mischievous gnomes, they never sleep.
They twist and turn, they hide, they play,
Guess my toes are not on display.

The crackling fire invites a snore,
As winter's games we can't ignore.
Chasing dreams while counting sheep,
This chilly season, oh so deep!

## A Hearth's Gentle Glow

The fire crackles, pops, and hisses,
Like a cat with its half-closed kisses.
Marshmallows dance on sticks of wood,
Oh wait, they're smoking, that's not good.

Sweaters hug like friends from school,
But why's my arm stuck? This isn't cool!
I twirl and spin in this knit embrace,
Searching for snacks, it's a tangled race.

We swap stories, laughter flies,
While frost creeps in with sneaky sighs.
A mug spills over, chocolate rivers flow,
Winter's chaos makes our hearts glow.

Under blankets, we play our game,
Who can stay warm, who takes the blame?
With every giggle, warmth returns,
In this cozy nest, my heart still yearns!

## Shades of Gray and White

Winter clouds hang low and tight,
Chasing away the sunny light.
But hey, I see a little fluff,
Maybe winter isn't so tough.

The ground is dressed in chilly white,
While I stumble in this funny fight.
My boots are stuck like they've befriend,
All of nature—what a blend!

Snowmen wink as they pass by,
With twiggy arms raised to the sky.
"Let's take a selfie!" they declare,
But that one's melting—I swear, I swear!

So let it snow, let giggles ring,
In wooly socks, we all can sing.
With shades of gray and white so bright,
This frosty season brings pure delight!

## The Glow of an Icy Hearth

The fireplace crackles bright,
As squirrels wear hats too tight.
Hot cocoa spills, a funny sight,
While snowflakes dance with pure delight.

The cat in slippers wobbles near,
Chasing shadows in sheer cheer.
The dog's in boots, oh what a gear,
As penguins mock, or so I hear.

Marshmallows float like little boats,
While snowmen wear our largest coats.
The cold invites us all to gloat,
With giggles bubbling, we take notes.

So let's toast to frosty cheer,
With smiles wide and no sad tear.
In this chill, the fun is clear,
As laughter warms us through the year.

## Winter's Gentle Sigh

Snowflakes tumble, oh what fun,
They tickle noses, nearly done.
Each breath a cloud, no need to run,
Winter whispers with a chilly pun.

The scarf wraps twice, it's quite a feat,
With mittens stuck, I can't compete.
Outside, children race on sleet,
While I sip tea, warm and sweet.

In hats too large, we prance around,
While slippery sidewalks claim the ground.
With every fall, the laughter's found,
A circus here, no need to frown.

So here's to snowball fights that spark,
In frozen worlds, we leave our mark.
With winter's sigh and joy to hark,
The season laughs, a playful lark.

## The Cuddle of the Cold Dawn

Mornings wrapped in frosty sheets,
Our blankets warm, but cold retreats.
Outside, the world's in icy feats,
While inside, giggles are receipts.

Fluffy socks on chilly toes,
Pancakes stack, a syrupy pose.
The sun peeks out, and laughter flows,
As snowmen strike a pose, who knows?

Frosted windows hide our grins,
As we pretend to winter win.
With snow-ball fights that lead to sins,
The joy in snow is where it begins.

With every turn, a funny sight,
The day unfolds with pure delight.
So hug the brisk and hold on tight,
For dawn brings play, and hearts take flight.

## Elysium of Snowdrifts

A kingdom built of fluffy white,
Where snowmen dance in pure delight.
With sleds that soar, and kites that kite,
Our laughter echoes, what a sight!

The carrot noses, all askew,
With twigs for arms, all cold and blue.
Yet still they wear a smile too,
As if they know just what to do.

The bunnies hop in coats of fluff,
While we gear up and bundle up.
With every slip, our giggles puff,
In this soft kingdom, not enough.

So let us laugh 'neath skies so gray,
In this elysium where we play.
With cups of cheer, we'll shout hooray,
For in the snow, we'll find our way.

## Echoes of the Frozen Wilderness

Snowflakes tumble, oh what a sight,
The penguin's dance, a comical flight.
Chilly cheeks and noses that glow,
Snowball battles, fast and low.

The squirrels wear hats made of ice,
Chattering loudly, aren't they precise?
A moose on skates, what a wild show,
He twirls and slips, oh no, oh no!

Frosty breath forms a cloud of glee,
As winter's antics set laughter free.
In the snowy woods, where fun takes flight,
We embrace the cold with sheer delight.

With mittens bright and scarves that twirl,
We laugh and play, give winter a whirl.
Echoes of joy through the frozen trees,
Winter's laughter rides on the breeze.

## Twilight in the Frosted Grove

Under the moon, the snowmen grin,
With carrot noses pointing like fins.
A snowball fight breaks out in swirl,
  As laughter dances, flags unfurl.

Frosty friends take a comical stance,
In twinkling lights, they start to prance.
The owls hoot with a wisecrack cheer,
  As winter's charm draws us near.

Glistening branches, a dazzling sight,
Rabbits jump high, oh what a flight!
In cozy corners, we sip hot stew,
Joy in the frost, just me and you.

Twilight whispers secrets untold,
As giggles ring out in the bitter cold.
With every flake, a moment to savor,
  Winter's giggle is our sweet favor.

# Lanterns in the Winter Night

Lanterns sway with a flickering glow,
Guiding my path through the crispy snow.
A raccoon rummages for a late snack,
While I dodge a snowdrift with a quick quack!

Snowflakes fall like confetti from the sky,
As deer join in, oh me, oh my!
With funny faces and silly leaps,
Their jolly frolic makes winter peep.

The chilly breeze carries tales anew,
Of penguins dancing, oh what a crew!
With laughter ringing through the deep night,
Frosted joy is a wonderful sight.

Twinkling lanterns mark our delight,
As winter plays, silly and bright.
We bundle up, with friends to delight,
In a world where laughter takes flight.

# A Tapestry of Glacial Hues

A patchwork quilt of icy blue,
As frosty fingers wave 'hello' to you.
The snowmen chat with a laugh and grin,
While chilly winds spin a playful din.

Carved in ice, the laughter glows,
As the winterflakes dance in winter shows.
A slippy slide for the dog's raucous race,
Oh my, what fun in this chilly place!

With fluffy hats and boots oversized,
We tumble and roll, oh what a surprise!
Hot cocoa spills while chuckles erupt,
Winter's embrace a cheerful corrupt.

Life under blankets, we giggle with cheer,
Wrapped in warmth, we have nothing to fear.
In glacial hues, we find our muse,
Winter's the canvas, we'll never lose.

Milton Keynes UK
Ingram Content Group UK Ltd.
UKHW022340171124
451242UK00007B/74